Other People

A play

Geoff Saunders

Samuel French—London
New York-Toronto-Hollywood

Please see page iv for further copyright information

OTHER PEOPLE

First performed by Group 64 at the Goodrich Theatre, Putney, London, on 8th November 1992, with the following cast:

Andrea	Gaëlle Hobbs
Stephen	Richard C. Broughton
Hilary	Sally James
Duncan	Jonathan Gambier

Directed by Geoff Saunders
With the assistance of Lesley Ann Thompson, David Jones and Dominic Banks

CHARACTERS

Andrea, early twenties
Stephen, early twenties
Hilary, slightly older
Duncan, early thirties

The action of the play takes place in the living-room of
the flat shared by Andrea, Stephen, Hilary and Duncan

Time—the present

To
Mum, Dad,
Michael, Katharine,
and
Christopher

... and to Caroline Ferris, who laughed
the loudest ...

OTHER PEOPLE

The living-room of the flat shared by Stephen, Andrea, Hilary and Duncan. 6.30 p.m. Winter

The room looks comfortable and warm, though the decor is dated and in need of renewal. The seating — armchairs and a sofa — is mismatched and rather shabby. A stereo unit features prominently, with a small table nearby. There are three doors: these lead to the entrance hall, the kitchen and to the rest of the flat

As the CURTAIN *rises, Stephen and Andrea are on stage. Stephen is sitting in an armchair reading a library book. He is in his early twenties and is rather scruffily dressed. Andrea is the same age and is, by contrast, very smartly dressed in casual, fashionable clothes. She is standing by the stereo unit, holding a record up to the light. A half-eaten Mars bar and a lighted cigarette rest on the table*

Andrea Oh God, oh God ...
Stephen Perhaps ——
Andrea Perhaps what?
Stephen Perhaps you should have been concentrating on what you were doing.
Andrea It wasn't my ... the needle just sort of fell out of my hand.
Stephen In which you also had a cigarette and a Mars bar.
Andrea (*scrutinizing the record*) It's not much of a scratch — only "Welcome to the Cruise" and "Sukarita".

Stephen Duncan's Judie Tzuke album!

Andrea Oh, no, it's one of his favourites, I suppose, don't tell me ...

Stephen Look at the sleeve.

Andrea What?

Stephen Look at the sleeve.

Andrea (*picking up the record sleeve and studying it closely*) Oh, Jesus.

Stephen Signed by the lady herself.

Andrea You had to point that out, didn't you? You're a right bastard, Stephen, you really are. Duncan's going to be furious.

Stephen Don't be daft, Duncan doesn't know how to be angry. You could gun down his entire family and he'd just say "Gosh".

Andrea But his favourite Judie Tzuke album ... Stephen, I've scratched it. What can I say to him?

Stephen Just tell him the truth.

Andrea That you made me laugh while I was putting the record on and ——

Stephen But I didn't ——

Andrea Yes, I know, but ——

Stephen I didn't make you laugh. I had nothing whatever to do with it. In fact, I don't remember saying a word to you. Deathlessly funny or otherwise.

Andrea But ——

Stephen You want me to share the blame, I suppose.

Andrea Can't you just say you told me a joke, or something? Distracted me? So I dropped the needle? He won't mind so much if he thinks you were involved. Duncan's your mate.

Stephen He's just as much yours as mine. More, in fact — you've lived here longer than I have. And that's beside the point, anyway. Whether I made you laugh or not, it was you who dropped the needle, you who scratched the record, Duncan's favourite Judie Tzuke album, signed by the lady herself at a concert in nineteen seventy-seven, you who ——

Andrea He'll hate me! Oh God, he'll hate me! Please, Steve, protect me. I don't want him to hate me.

Stephen But you wouldn't mind if he hated us both? Eh? You wouldn't mind lousing up my friendship with him as well?

Andrea Oh, that's right, that's fine, that is, yes, go ahead, save yourself! You never own up to anything, do you? It's always my fault, isn't it? Something's gone wrong, let's blame Andrea! You must really hate me too! Well, I can't blame you for that, really. I hate myself too, a lot of the time. I've always been awkward, clumsy, you know. When I was seven I got water in my ears and it affected my balance and I was forever falling over. Just as that was clearing up I kept on being sick. I was sick in the font at St Peter's once. And in the library at school, three times, twice in the Biology section and once in Home Economics. My father was horrible to me about that. He kept making jokes about how a pool of sick was hardly an advertisement for the cookery books.

Stephen sniggers

Oh, thank you so much! I need my cigarette. (*She picks up her cigarette. It has gone out*) Oh, no! No! (*Almost in tears, she rummages through her pockets until she finds her lighter. She lights the cigarette, inhales desperately, then seems to become calmer*) It was humiliating. I carried a plastic bag around with me for nearly five years just in case. The doctors did every test under the sun and the only conclusion they could come to was that it was psychosomatic. Well, of course, from then on, my mother was convinced I was loopy. Which wasn't — isn't — too far from the truth, I suppose. So, you see, it doesn't surprise me at all that you hate me. I'm used to it. But I do think you could try to understand me. If you just knew what I'd been through ...

Stephen But I do know. I know very well.

Andrea How can you? How can you know?

Stephen Because you've told me. Ad infi-bloody-nitum.

There is the sound of a door opening, off, then footsteps

Andrea He's here! Please, Steve, what can I say? What can I tell him?

Stephen I've told you. Tell him the truth.

Andrea I can't. He'll hate me.

Stephen He won't. He doesn't know what hatred is. There's also the chance he might think you're not worth the effort, seeing as you hate yourself enough for the both of you.

Andrea Please, Steve, help me, he's coming!

Stephen Tell him the truth. And if you lie, I won't support you.

Andrea You're a selfish bastard, Stephen Adams, you really are. (*She grabs the Mars bar and retreats across the room, away from the hall door*)

Hilary enters from the hall. She is slightly older than the others and wears an immaculate business suit. She is carrying a brief-case and a wet raincoat

Hilary Hi. I've left my umbrella to dry in the hallway, don't fall over it.

Andrea Oh, it's you.

Hilary Indeed.

Andrea I thought — we thought — we thought it was Duncan. But it's you. Thank God it's you.

Hilary Well it's nice to be appreciated, even if it's just for not being somebody else. Stephen, the coat-hooks in the hallway ...

Stephen Oh, no, I'm sorry.

Hilary You've been here all day. It only takes half an hour to put up a few coat-hooks.

Stephen I'll do it tomorrow.

Hilary Well, do. Now that it's raining all the time we need them. There's nothing worse than having wet raincoats all over the place.

Andrea Hilary, I've got a problem.

Hilary Well, well, doesn't that make a change. Our flatmate has a problem.

Andrea Please, Hilary.

Hilary Just let me hang my coat up in the kitchen and I'll be with you. (*She heads for the kitchen*)

Andrea Just a minute ago I was going to put a record on — some old Judie Tzuke thing of Duncan's — and Steve told me this really funny joke and ——

Hilary exits into the kitchen

Hilary (*off*) My God!

Andrea Hilary?

Hilary (*off*) This room was spotless when I left this morning. Spotless!

She enters, furious

All the mugs were clean, the table was clean, for once, and the floor was clean; I even made myself late for work scrubbing that ruddy floor!

Andrea Hilary ...

Hilary Eileen Cathcart said: "Why are you late, Hilary Johnson?" and when I told her ——

Andrea Hilary! This is really important!

Hilary When I told her I'd had to clean the floor because I knew no-one else would do it and I couldn't bear the thought of it being so filthy all day while I was at work, do you know what she did?

Andrea Please Hil, it is important.

Hilary So's this, Andrea.

Stephen What did she do, Hilary?

Hilary She laughed in my face, the cow. Laughed in my face. She's a heartless bitch. It's easy for her, of course, she has a cleaning lady.

Stephen All the same you can hardly blame her for laughing, can you? It is pretty ridiculous.

Andrea Look I'm sorry, but ——

Hilary Ridiculous, is it? To want to live in a clean and tidy flat where you don't have to do a mountain of washing-up before making a cup of coffee, where you don't ——

Andrea Please Hilary ——

Hilary Oh, for heaven's sake Andrea! Look, I'm sorry Stephen, I know it's different for people who've been to university, where being untidy and unhygienic is thought of as creative and trendy ——

Andrea Please!

Hilary — and somehow the mark of true intellect, but I didn't go to university and even if I had I might well have grown out of those habits a long time ago.

Andrea Will someone please listen to me? Oh God, no-one ever listens to me!

Stephen Oh but they do, Andrea. They do. I reckon you'd have grown up a hell of a sight sooner if you'd been ignored a few times.

Hilary I'm going to tidy up the kitchen now. (*She heads for the kitchen*) I don't know how I've survived in this madhouse for so long.

Andrea (*following Hilary*) Please don't be angry with me, Hilary, you know what I'm like, I need support, I always have.

Hilary And always will. Look, you know I care about you and I'll never turn you down when you need help ——

Andrea Oh, Hilary, you are lovely. (*She hugs Hilary*)

Hilary (*extricating herself*) — but at this moment I am in a pig of a bad mood — I even said the "f" word at work today, I'm so ashamed — so my first priority is to tidy up the kitchen and get rid of my aggressive feelings, otherwise ——

Andrea But this is really urgent ——

Hilary — otherwise I may well break your neck. Look, I can hardly unclench my fists. Discuss whatever it is with Stephen. He fancies

himself as a philosopher. I'll take over when I've calmed down
a bit.

Hilary exits into the kitchen

Stephen J. P. Sartre was right. Hell is other people.
Hilary (*off*) What was that?
Stephen Oh nothing much.
Andrea Steve, I'm so unhappy ...
Stephen I keep telling myself that days like this — well, evenings
like this, the days are bliss on my own — I keep telling myself that
evenings like this are the exception. But they're not. All I've ever
wanted is the proverbial quiet life, and what have I got? Dante's
bleedin' Inferno. Dante's bleedin' Inferno twice nightly with
quadruple helpings of rage and hand-wringing. Some people
would find it amusing, I suppose, entertaining even, but it
knackers me out.
Andrea Are you being funny?

*There is the sound of the front door opening, then footsteps, then the
sound of someone falling over*

Duncan (*off*) Oh, dear.
Andrea He's here! Steve, he's here! (*She moves as far away from
the hall door as possible*)

Hilary enters at a run

Hilary Duncan, my umbrella's ...

Hilary disappears into the hallway.

(*Off*) Oh, I'm sorry, Duncan, are you all right?
Duncan (*off*) Yes, I'm fine. No bones broken. Umbrellas's all right,
too, I think.

Hilary (*off*) I left it there to dry off a bit.

Duncan (*off*) No, really don't worry. I'm perfectly all right.

Hilary (*off*) It was really silly of me. I should have left the light on.

Duncan (*off*) Don't concern yourself. There's no need to fuss over me.

Duncan enters with Hilary. Duncan is in his early thirties and is staidly dressed in a dark suit and conservative tie. He carries a briefcase and a wet raincoat

Not that I'd accuse you of fussing. No, I appreciate your concern. Hallo, Stephen, Andrea.

Stephen Hi.

Andrea Duncan ——

Duncan Fell over Hilary's umbrella. Don't think I've broken it.

Andrea Duncan, look I'm really sorry, but ——

Hilary Right. (*She heads for the kitchen, then turns back to Duncan*) You're sure you're all right, Duncan?

Duncan Positive.

Hilary Good. Well, I'll get on.

Duncan Right.

Hilary Just give me your coat and I'll hang it up to dry in here.

Hilary takes Duncan's wet coat and exits into the kitchen

(*Off*) Someone was going to put up some hooks in the hallway, but someone forgot.

Stephen I said I'd ——

Andrea (*to Duncan*) Oh, this is awful. Look, Duncan, we're friends, aren't we?

Duncan Oh! Well, er, I've never ——

Andrea It's just that ... I can't, I can't — Steve, you tell him.

Stephen You're joking!

Andrea I can't. I feel so awful.

Stephen So what? It has nothing to do with me!

Andrea You said you'd help me! You said you'd support me!

Stephen Did I? Did I say that ? I don't think I did.

Duncan Andrea, Stephen, it's all right. Whatever it is, I'm sure it's not worth all this.

Andrea Stephen, please, I can't get through this on my own!

Stephen Oh, for Christ's sake! Duncan, Andrea scratched your Judie Tzuke album.

Duncan Oh, that's ——

Andrea The one she signed herself! Don't hate me, Duncan, I know that album's important to you, and precious, but I didn't mean it, I just dropped the needle ... (*She bursts into tears*)

Duncan No honestly, don't cry, it's only a record.

Andrea But she signed it! I'm so sorry to have hurt you. Please forgive me.

Duncan There's nothing to forgive, honestly. Accidents will happen. And I'm not hurt, please don't cry.

Andrea You're such a good person, Duncan. You make me feel so petty and stupid and ... bad. Which I am, of course. Please say you forgive me. Please say it.

Duncan Really, it doesn't matter. It doesn't. It's nothing.

Andrea Just say it!

Duncan Andrea ——

Andrea It wasn't just me, you know. I was being careful, really concentrating, and Steve told this really funny joke that just——

Stephen How could you! You little ... (*To Duncan*) That bit's not true at all.

Andrea It put me off for a moment and I dropped the needle. I'm so sorry, Duncan, I'm ... Oh, God, you really hate us, don't you? Don't hate us please, we're your friends, we didn't mean it.

She rushes from the room, overcome with emotion, through the door that leads to the rest of the flat

Duncan Oh dear, she's terribly upset.

Stephen And why aren't you?

Duncan Me? No, it doesn't matter.

Stephen It does. I know it does. I can remember you telling me how excited you were the day you met Judie Tzuke at that concert. And she signed the album you'd just bought. And you also said that album was one of your prized possessions.

Duncan Well, it is.

Stephen You're not upset?

Duncan No.

Hilary appears in the kitchen doorway and stands listening

Stephen You're lying. You're angry but you don't want trouble so you're lying.

Duncan I'm sorry, Stephen, but not I'm not angry. Even if I was I wouldn't show it. Andrea's young, lonely, vulnerable; who am I to add to her troubles?

Stephen Oh, now we're St Francis of bloody Assisi, are we? I suppose you're going to say next that you understand her?

Duncan Well, I ——

Stephen People like you always understand, or say that you do. It saves you from having to judge anyone, saves you from having to get off your cowardly little backsides and say "I believe this", to make a commitment to anything. You know, I reckon Andrea would be a much better person if only a few people would challenge her, make her aware of the consequences of her actions, but, oh, no, everyone understands her, so she gets away with murder. Only God understands, right? You're as un-bloody-saintly as the rest of us so why not admit it and stand up for yourself?

Duncan That's very unkind, Stephen. I don't deserve such an attack. I'll think about it though.

Stephen Don't think about it, fight! Argue! Behave like a young person for once.

Duncan I'm over thirty now, Stephen. I'm trying to behave maturely.

Stephen So you're judging me now are you? Saying I'm immature?
Duncan You said it yourself: I don't judge. (*A slight smile*) If the cap fits, however, as they say...

Duncan exits through the door to the rest of the flat

Hilary You handled that beautifully, Stephen.
Stephen You can piss off too! (*He smiles*) God, it's got me, too. Now I'm ranting and raving like everyone else. He just makes me so mad. Andrea makes our lives a bloody misery with her tantrums and carelessness and endless apologizing and he doesn't lift a finger to oppose her. Did you hear all that about his record?
Hilary Every word. Just typical. Perversely enough, though, I admire Duncan's cool, his ability to keep things in proportion. I tend to fly off the handle at the slightest thing, like the kitchen earlier.
Stephen But it's unhealthy, it's wrong, keeping your feelings bottled up like he does.
Hilary It isn't for him.
Stephen He should have made her realize that she's got to face her responsibilities, that she has no right to spoil his things.
Hilary But if it doesn't matter to him, why should he? Surely, he has the right to respond to the situation in his own way. (*Pause*) I'm getting philosophical. That's the trouble with this flat. We're all too bloody analytical and clever about everything. We'd probably all get on much better if we weren't so articulate.
Stephen It takes an articulate person to worry about being articulate. I like the irony.

There is a lengthy pause. Stephen resumes his library book. Hilary sits down, takes her shoes off and shuts her eyes for a moment. Silence

Hilary (*quietly*) The rent is due.
Stephen Tough.

Hilary Did you read Mr Craven's letter?

Stephen It was addressed to you.

Hilary So you didn't read it. Well he said we've got to be more punctual with the rent or there'll be trouble.

Stephen I can't pay it. Not this month.

Hilary What do you mean, can't?

Stephen I don't get rent support for another three weeks. Or the dole.

Hilary So what do we tell Mr Craven, eh? He specifically asks for employed people when he's advertising this place.

Stephen Well, I was working when I started here. It's not my fault I was asked to leave.

Hilary Sacked.

Stephen Made redundant.

Hilary Sacked.

Stephen All right then, sacked.

Hilary For idleness.

Stephen Hold on ——

Hilary And what's the betting you haven't even started looking for a new job?

Stephen Well ——

Hilary Don't try to kid me! You've spent the entire month lolling around here watching children's TV and Australian soaps and eating my bloody food!

Stephen I haven't eaten your food!

Hilary You have! Where did that quiche go then? Eh? And that Marks and Sparks lasagne?

Stephen I'm sorry.

Hilary That's all right. The lasagne was well past its sell-by date anyway. Joke. Great. So you've not so much as started job-hunting and you don't have any money. So thanks to you, Mr Craven will go completely mad, especially as you and Andrea have been late with the rent every month since I can't remember when — and he'll probably ask us to leave.

Stephen He can't.

Hilary He can. If you'd bothered to read his letter you'd have seen he hints very strongly that this is the last time he'll accept late cheques and lame excuses.

Stephen Well, I genuinely can't pay.

Hilary So he'll genuinely have to get rid of you. And the rest of us as well, for causing him so much hassle.

Stephen You and Duncan are always on time with your rent.

Hilary True, but I know these people. If one person in a flat gets into trouble the landlord blames everyone and out they all go. Consider Alison and Donald Aitchison ...

Stephen God, yes ...

There is a pause

Hilary So you're not going to do anything?

Stephen Like what? What can I do?

Hilary Ask your parents to bail you out.

Stephen No way. They washed their hands of me ages ago.

Hilary Well, I can hardly blame them for that. But this is an emergency. Surely ——

Stephen No, look, I'll talk to Mr Craven. I'll reason with him.

Hilary You can't reason with him. He's a landlord, a lower form of life, with the rational faculties of pond slime.

Stephen You don't like him much, do you?

Hilary And there I was, thinking I was masking my true emotions perfectly. No I don't. And, to be honest, I'm pretty un-fond of you at the moment, as you're endangering our tenure of this flat.

Stephen I'm unemployed, right? I have no money, right? I don't need any grief from you!

Hilary Then don't give me any.

Stephen I'll talk to Mr Craven.

Hilary Please do. Soon.

Duncan enters

Duncan I'm going to have a bath, if that's all right. Anyone who
wants to use the loo had better do so now.

Stephen Righto. Thanks Duncan, you timed that very well; I was
beginning to buckle under the onslaught.

Duncan I'm sorry?

Stephen Hilary's doing her rent–police bit. Part of her Gestapo
training.

Stephen exits through the door to the rest of the flat

Hilary See? I turn on my best professionally cheerful manner and
what happens? He still gets upset. Damn. (*She pauses*) Would it
surprise you, Duncan, that I was Head Girl at school? And a senior
prefect before that, library monitor before that and even at
primary school, milk monitor? I, and I alone, was allowed to put
the straws in the milk bottles and carry the crate round the
classroom. I've been an organizer all my life, God alone knows
why. My family's completely disorganized. Grandparents, parents, both my brothers, totally hopeless. Late for everything,
never looking tidy, never knowing what they're supposed to be
doing. All having a wonderful time. And in the middle of it, me,
desperately organizing things: meal times, bedtimes, cleaning
shoes, worrying, worrying, worrying about having the right
dinner money or whether my hair had been brushed enough times.
And wanting, more than anything, to be able to let go, have fun,
be a mess, be late without caring. But, somewhere in my family's
past, a little, miserable organizing gene was introduced into the
line, and, having skipped a few generations, blossomed with
knobs on in me. I hate it. I hate having red hands because I wash
them all the time, I hate the attacks of breathlessness I get if I miss
the bus, I hate making myself late for work because I've had to run
home and change my ear-rings because they don't co-ordinate
with my skirt. I hate it. It drives me mad.

Pause

Duncan I've ... er ... I've written out my rent cheque. You can have it this evening.

Hilary I feel so guilty about Andrea. She needs so much support and I've always been able to give it to her in the past. But tonight — tonight I couldn't. I've had an awful day, Duncan, one of the worst. I've been dumped on all day: "Hilary, can you just do this for me?", "Hilary, can I talk this through with you?" Erica Bisley can't decide whether to have an abortion and spent three quarters of an hour in my office, crying, which is fine, but I was supposed to be able to give her sympathy, help, support, you name it, and deal with the monthly accounting which had to be done by four. To come home and find Andrea doing her drowning puppy routine and getting ready to dump all her problems on me was the last straw. I do feel sorry for her, I even like her, but, tonight, well, I could happily have shoved her in the microwave and run away laughing. Which is an awful thing to think about anyone.

Pause. Duncan looks distinctly uncomfortable

Thank you for having your cheque ready, anyway, Duncan. It's nice that there's one person here I can rely on.

Andrea enters

Which is more than can be said of ——

Andrea Were you talking about me?

Hilary I was about to be phenomenally rude about you, Andrea, but you ruined everything by turning up.

Andrea Oh.

Hilary Never mind. I'm sure another opportunity will present itself. It normally does. At the moment, the most important matter is the rent.

Andrea The rent?

Hilary It's due. I don't suppose you read Mr Craven's letter?

Andrea It had your name on it.

Hilary You lot are hopeless, you really are. Anything from Mr Craven will be for all of us, not just me, it stands to reason. Initiative is dead, long live apathy.

Andrea I can't pay.

Hilary Anyway, if you'd bothered to read his letter, you'd know that he's getting fed up with us constantly being late with the rent and ... what did you say?

Andrea I can't pay it.

Hilary This I don't believe.

Andrea Well, not all of it, anyway. I just don't have enough.

Hilary Oh brilliant. Mr Craven's going to have us all out before you can say "tenancy agreement".

Andrea Out?

Hilary Out. Evicted. On the street. If we don't pay. If *you* don't pay.

Andrea It's not my fault! You can't blame it on me!

Hilary Where's the money gone then, eh? Were you robbed?

Andrea No.

Hilary You're being blackmailed by someone who knows you have a facial hair problem?

Andrea No.

Duncan (*to Andrea*) Do you?

Andrea You keep out of this!

Hilary Duncan, please don't change the subject!

Duncan Sorry.

Hilary Well?

There is a pause. Andrea looks shamefaced

(*Light dawning*) That dress you wore to Katy's party ...

Andrea It was reduced.

Hilary To what?

Andrea Look, Hilary, I was really depressed. I had to cheer myself up somehow. I hadn't stopped crying for two days ——

Hilary As if I don't remember. How much?

Andrea — and I saw it in this shop window and I thought to myself, "That'll cheer me up! I'll buy it, however much it costs."

Hilary Andrea!

Andrea Well, I felt I was worth it!

Duncan It is a very pretty dress.

Hilary Thank you, Duncan. Andrea?

Andrea A hundred and seventy-five pounds.

Hilary And you paid cash.

Andrea (*beginning to cry*) My credit cards were stopped last month. And I'm four hundred pounds over my overdraft limit now.

Hilary You are a stupid, selfish little cow!

Andrea I'm sorry, I'm really sorry. I was so depressed. I had to do something. I know it was silly, but it did cheer me up for a while.

Hilary A couple of drinks would have had the same effect and cost considerably less! My God, you've really achieved classic status this time. One stupid, hideous, tarty ——

Andrea You said you liked it!

Hilary — overpriced little frock and four people get made homeless!

Andrea Don't, please, Hilary, you're hurting me! I'm sorry. I really am. Please forgive me. I'll feel awful if you don't forgive me.

Hilary How can I?

Andrea Duncan, you forgive me, don't you?

Duncan Well, gosh ... of course, Andrea, of course I do. No harm done.

Andrea See, Hilary: Duncan forgives me.

Hilary Oh, does he now. Well, I don't. God, it's all so easy for you isn't it? You spend half your time being a pain and the other half asking to be forgiven for being a pain, which is a pain in itself, and everything's meant to be all right. What you never do is make any bloody effort not to be a pain in the first place; you think that apologizing will make it all better. Until next time. Well, your apologies stink, Andrea. They mean nothing.

Andrea You hate me, don't you? You've always hated me. All of you! You've never even made an effort to like me!

Duncan begins to edge towards the door leading to the rest of the flat

Hilary (*to Andrea*) Well, you've never made any effort to be likeable! (*She sees Duncan moving away*) Where are you going?
Duncan My bath ...
Hilary Stephen's in there! Don't run away, I need a witness!
Duncan Oh, but, er ——
Hilary Stephen's right! You're a complete moral coward!
Andrea Don't be horrible to Duncan!
Hilary Why the hell not?
Andrea He's the only one of you who's ever shown me any kindness.
Hilary Only because he's too bloody frightened of you to say no!
Andrea That's enough, Hilary, please!
Hilary I'm wasting my breath here, I can tell.
Andrea This is just awful, awful! I don't need this in my life! I've been so happy here and now you've ruined it! Ruined it!

Andrea exits through the door to the rest of the flat. There is a considerable pause

Stephen enters

Stephen Good heavens, here's a surprise: Andrea's crying. I'm amazed this flat isn't flooded on a regular basis with her here.
Hilary Duncan, you heard her; she likes you. Could you talk to her about the rent? You work in a bank, after all; surely you know of some way she can sort herself out?
Duncan Well, I'd rather not, actually ... you see ——
Hilary Why not?
Duncan Well, she's so upset, she's very fragile ...

Hilary You saw the letter, Duncan. No rent, no flat. Craven is sick to death of us. Please just talk to her.

Duncan I couldn't; she'd only get more upset. I'm no good at that sort of thing anyway. I prefer not to get involved.

Hilary You are the completest mouse, aren't you? I've never known such a coward!

Duncan It isn't cowardice, not at all. I just happen to believe that it's more ... mature ... to leave people to make up their own minds about things.

Stephen You're mature then, are you Duncan? Is never having an opinion mature? Is never taking responsibility for anything mature? Is running away from any emotional confrontation mature?

Duncan One has to learn to let people live their own lives in their own way.

Stephen You pompous git!

Duncan Was that mature?

Stephen I've never claimed to be mature. In fact, I'm quite glad now that I'm not. If being mature means being a spineless, character-less nonentity like you, I want to be a child forever!

Hilary Don't worry, Stephen, you will. Now, chaps before we get into round two of this fascinating moral debate, can we please discuss the rent problem?

Stephen You're calling a meeting?

Hilary Well, no, not exactly, but we've got to do something haven't we?

Stephen You mean *you've* got to do something. You're taking charge.

Hilary No, not at all.

Stephen Why do you always take charge, eh? Suddenly you're the flat's rent collector and bully, and no-one asked you to be.

Hilary If I didn't do it, who would? Duncan's afraid to ask anyone for so much as a penny, you're too bloody idle and Andrea would probably burst into tears at the thought. It's got to be me.

Stephen But why does anyone have to do it? We're here collectively.

Hilary Not in the political sense.

Stephen All right, no, but ... well, we are all, supposedly, equal: why should one person have to take responsibility for any one task?

Hilary Because if she didn't — note I say she because it's always me, isn't it — if she didn't no-one else would and we'd be out on our ears.

Stephen Typical fascist scare-mongering tactics, those ...

Hilary My God, you can be so stupid sometimes! Mr Craven has every right to throw us out!

Stephen Perhaps he has, but that doesn't give you the right to lord it over everyone else.

Hilary One day you'll stop being clever and start being intelligent; then you'll realize what a prize pillock you've been for the past twenty-odd years. You don't do anything, you just sit about making smart comments and picking holes in other people. You make me sick.

Duncan Hilary!

Hilary (*to Duncan*) And so do you! You may be St Francis of Assisi in terms of maturity but you're positively Neanderthal in every other respect. (*She pauses*) Right, I've had enough of this. I'm going to clear up the kitchen.

Hilary exits into the kitchen. She returns almost immediately

No. I'm not. Why the hell should I?

Duncan No, that's fine, Hilary, I'm happy to do it.

Hilary You didn't make the mess.

Duncan No, but I feel a bit guilty, really; perhaps I should help you out a bit more.

Hilary Great. Now I'm responsible for making people feel guilty. And, Duncan, it's not a case of helping me by clearing up, it's a

case of doing your fair share. The sooner you people stop thinking
of me as the housekeeper who has, occasionally, to be honoured
with help, the better. We are, as Stephen points out, a collective;
this should mean but doesn't, as yet, that everything is shared
equally, including the cleaning. After all, I can't be the only one
who doesn't like living in a pigsty.

Stephen My God, you're terrifying! Mess really offends you,
doesn't it? Any kind of disorder offends your tidy middle-class,
middle-aged, anally-retentive mind!

Hilary Whose crockery is that on the draining board? And that
teapot? I mean, to whom do they actually belong?

Stephen Well, they're mine actually, why?

Hilary Right.

*Hilary storms off into the kitchen. A series of crockery smashes is
heard, continuing under the following dialogue*

(*Off*) Here's some mess for you! Clear this bloody lot up yourself!

Stephen (*rushing to the kitchen door*) What the hell are you doing?

Hilary (*off*) You wanted a mess? Here's a mess! It's all yours!

Stephen That's my stuff you're breaking! Leave it!

Stephen exits into the kitchen

*The smashing noises stop; then there is the sound of a very loud slap
and a cry from Stephen*

Stephen enters from the kitchen, clutching his cheek

She bloody hit me! She's gone mad! Completely mad!

*The crashing continues. Hilary is screaming, off, half with joy, half
with rage. Stephen stands near the door watching her. Duncan
retreats into a corner*

Andrea enters

Andrea Oh no, what's happening?
Duncan Hilary's upset. She's smashing up the kitchen.
Andrea Stop it, Hilary! Stop it! You're making me feel awful! I
  would have washed up, I really would have, but I was so upset I
  just couldn't. Stop it, Hilary, please stop it! I've said I'm sorry.
  (*She falls into an armchair and curls up, weeping noisily*) I'm
  sorry, I'm sorry! Oh, God, I hate you ! I hate you! I hate you all!

There are more crashes. Then silence

*Hilary, dishevelled and exhausted, emerges from the kitchen and
stands wearily in the doorway*

The others all look at Hilary

Hilary smiles

CURTAIN

FURNITURE AND PROPERTY LIST

Only essential furniture and properties are listed here. Further dressing may be added at the director's discretion

On stage: Armchairs
Sofa
Stereo unit
Table. *On it:* half-eaten Mars bar, lighted cigarette, record sleeve
Library book for **Stephen**
Record for **Andrea**

Off stage: Raincoat (**Hilary**)
Briefcase (**Hilary**)
Raincoat (**Duncan**)
Briefcase (**Duncan**)

Personal: **Andrea**: lighter

LIGHTING PLOT

Property fittings required: nil
Interior. The same scene throughout

To open: General interior lighting

No cues

EFFECTS PLOT

No cues